21084

Team Spirit

THE TORONTO RAPTORS

BY

MARK STEWART

Content Consultant
Matt Zeysing
Historian and Archivist
The Naismith Memorial Basketball Hall of Fame

CHICAGO, ILLINOIS

Norwood House Press
P.O. Box 316598
Chicago, Illinois 60631

For information regarding Norwood House Press, please visit our website at:
www.norwoodhousepress.com or call 866-565-2900.

All photos courtesy of Getty Images except the following:
Topps, Inc. (9, 14, 35 top left & right, 36, 43),
Toronto Raptors (16, 34 left), Matt Richman (48).
Cover Photo: Barry Gossage/Getty Images
Special thanks to Topps, Inc.

Editor: Mike Kennedy
Designer: Ron Jaffe
Project Management: Black Book Partners, LLC.
Research: Joshua Zaffos

Library of Congress Cataloging-in-Publication Data

Stewart, Mark, 1960-
    The Toronto Raptors / by Mark Stewart ; content consultant, Matt Zeysing.
        p. cm. -- (Team spirit)
    Includes bibliographical references and index.
    Summary: "Presents the history and accomplishments of the Toronto
Raptors basketball team. Includes highlights of players, coaches, and awards,
quotes, timelines, maps, glossary and websites"--Provided by publisher.
    ISBN-13: 978-1-59953-292-9 (library edition : alk. paper)
    ISBN-10: 1-59953-292-1 (library edition : alk. paper) 1. Toronto Raptors
(Basketball team)--History--Juvenile literature. 2.
Basketball--Ontario--Toronto--History--Juvenile literature. I. Zeysing,
Matt. II. Title.
    GV885.52.T67S73 2009
    796.323'640975924--dc22
                                                        2008044304

Manufactured in the United States of America.

COVER PHOTO: The Raptors get fired up before a game during the 2007–08 season.

Table of Contents

SPORTS WORDS & VOCABULARY WORDS: In this book, you will find many words that are new to you. You may also see familiar words used in new ways. The glossary on page 46 gives the meanings of basketball words, as well as "everyday" words that have special basketball meanings. These words appear in **bold type** throughout the book. The glossary on page 47 gives the meanings of vocabulary words that are not related to basketball. They appear in ***bold italic type*** throughout the book.

BASKETBALL SEASONS: Because each basketball season begins late in one year and ends early in the next, seasons are not named after years. Instead, they are written out as two years separated by a dash, for example 1944–45 or 2005–06.

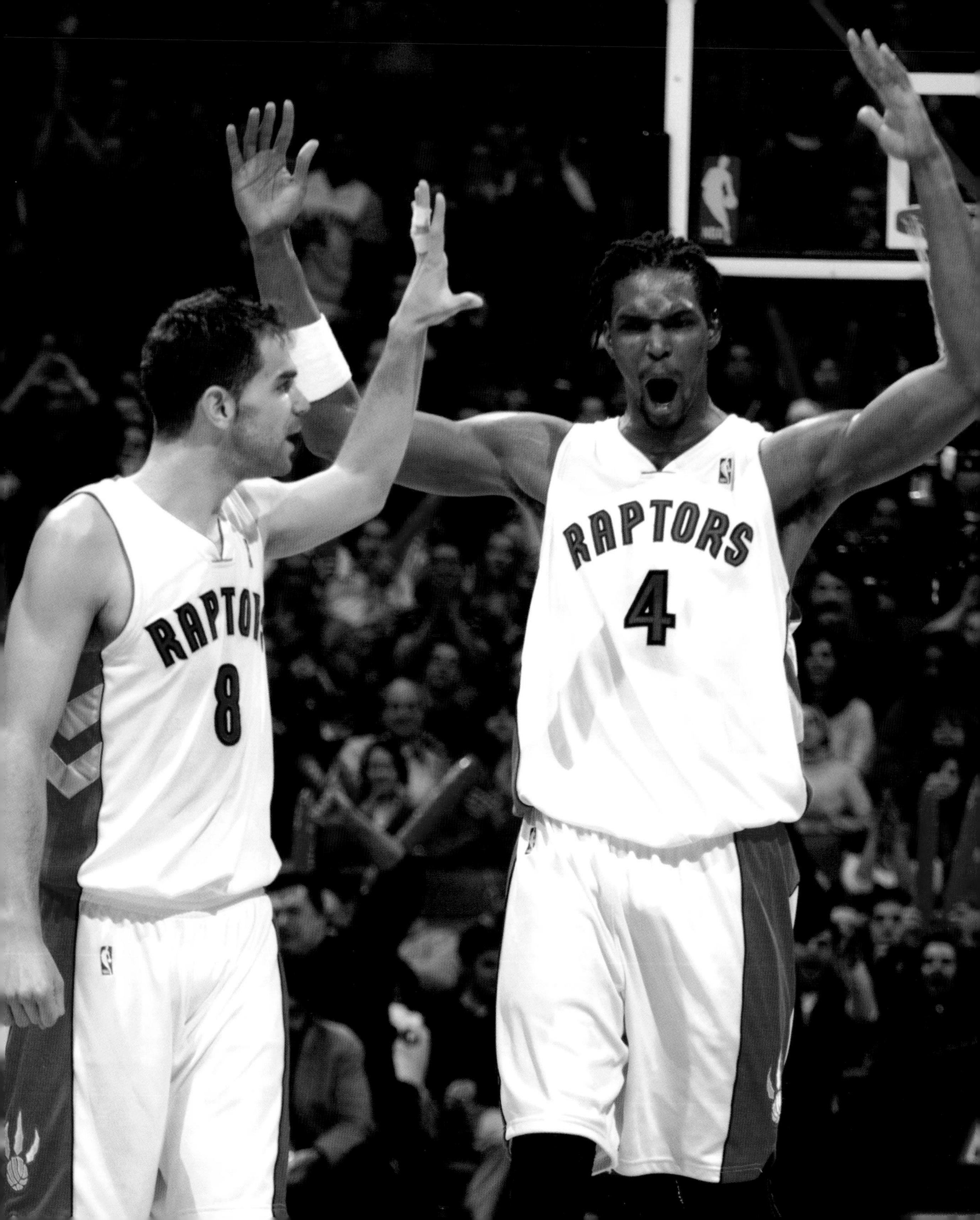
RAPTORS
8
RAPTORS
4

Meet the Raptors

Any scientist will tell you that the age of the dinosaur ended millions of years ago. Basketball fans in Toronto might disagree. As far as they are concerned, the best is yet to come for their team, the Raptors. The club has given its fans many thrills over the years in its quest for a **National Basketball Association (NBA)** championship.

The Raptors look for players who have unusual talent. The challenge for the team's coaches is finding the right way to blend these skills. Toronto hopes to create problems for opponents that are used to playing against other teams. The Raptors always try to do the unexpected.

This book tells the story of the Raptors. They play their best when they have strong, talented leaders—and they have had some good ones over the years. Will the team find the right combination and compete for a championship? All it takes is hard work, smart play, and a few lucky bounces.

Jose Calderon congratulates Chris Bosh after a great play during a 2007–08 game.

Way Back When

Basketball was red-hot in the 1990s. The game had more fans in more places than ever before. The NBA wanted to bring its version of the sport into Canada. The Toronto Raptors were one of two **expansion teams** formed for the 1995–96 season. The Vancouver Grizzlies, in Western Canada, were the NBA's other new club.

The Raptors built their team with the help of Isiah Thomas. He had just retired from the Detroit Pistons. Thomas had been an **All-Star**

during his career. He knew talent when he saw it. The Raptors found many good players, including Tracy Murray, Alvin Robertson, and Oliver Miller. One of the stars that Thomas brought to Toronto was his old teammate John Salley. They had won two championships together in Detroit.

The Raptors put their team in the hands of their first **draft choice**, Damon Stoudamire. He stood just 5′ 10″, but he loved to attack the defense. His courageous drives to the basket helped him lead the Raptors in points and **assists**. The team finished the year with 21 victories.

The Raptors improved to 30 wins in their second season. The difference was defense. **Rookie** Marcus Camby gave the Raptors a shot-blocker at center, and Doug Christie could cover the league's high-scoring guards. One of the teams the Raptors beat was the Chicago Bulls. It was one of only 13 losses for the Bulls that year.

Toronto's future looked bright. In 1997–98, the Raptors decided to give their young players a chance to play. They relied heavily on Tracy McGrady. At 18, he was the youngest player in the NBA. One year later, McGrady was joined by

Vince Carter. Toronto traded for Carter on the day of the **NBA draft**. By the 1999–00 season, the Raptors had added three experienced stars to their front line, Kevin Willis, Charles Oakley, and Antonio Davis. The team won 45 games and made the **playoffs** for the first time.

LEFT: Isiah Thomas and Damon Stoudamire
ABOVE: Tracy McGrady soars for a dunk.

Carter was the star of the show for Toronto. His scoring, dunking, and warm smile reminded many of Michael Jordan. For three years in a row, Carter had more votes for the **All-Star Game** than anyone else in the NBA. Fans flocked to see "Vinsanity" wherever he played. At home, the Raptors were setting new records for tickets sold.

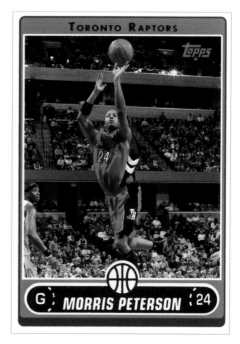

To take the step from being a good team to being a great one, the Raptors had to make a move. Because Carter and McGrady played the same position, Toronto decided to trade McGrady. But instead of competing for a championship, the Raptors struggled to win half their games. Injuries were part of the problem. Mostly, though, it was a lack of **team chemistry**.

Toronto fans never knew what to expect of the Raptors from one night to the next. They put good players on the court, including Hakeem Olajuwon, Dell Curry, Morris Peterson, Jerome Williams, Jalen Rose, and Donyell Marshall. However, they lacked the spirit of the earlier clubs. In 2004, Carter asked the Raptors to trade him. It was the end of one *era* for Toronto, but also the beginning of another.

LEFT: Vince Carter rises for a jump shot. With the Raptors, he became one of the league's most popular players.
ABOVE: A trading card of Morris Peterson.

The Team Today

The day Vince Carter left the Raptors, Chris Bosh became the team's new leader. Although he was only 20, the **upbeat** forward understood how to bring his older teammates together. The Raptors surrounded Bosh with smart, unselfish players. In no time, Toronto rediscovered its winning ways.

The Raptors **outsmarted** other NBA teams by finding talent in unusual places. Toronto signed a number of foreign players, including Jose Calderon, Andrea Bargnani, and Roko Ukic. The Raptors benefited greatly from the addition of *international* stars. No team was more fun to watch and root for.

Toronto wasn't finished building a new team for the 21st *century*. By adding well-known stars such as Jermaine O'Neal, Jason Kapono, and Anthony Parker, the Raptors assembled a **roster** of players that could win in many different ways. Fans in Toronto had a reason to celebrate. They knew that something exciting was brewing.

Jermaine O'Neal and Chris Bosh walk off the court during the 2008–09 season. They gave the Raptors a great one-two scoring punch.

11

Home Court

The Raptors' first home was Toronto's famous SkyDome, which is now called the Rogers Centre. SkyDome featured a **retractable** roof, the Hard Rock Cafe, and a hotel with 70 rooms that **overlooked** the court. The Raptors' largest crowd at SkyDome was 36,131 for a 1996 game against the Chicago Bulls.

The Raptors moved into a new arena during the 1998–99 season. The building is owned by the same company that owns the Raptors and hockey's Toronto Maple Leafs. The first sponsor of the arena was an airline company called Air Canada. So of course, fans nicknamed it the "Hangar." The arena is famous for its many restaurants and food stands, which reflect the great **cultural diversity** of the city.

BY THE NUMBERS

- *The Raptors' arena has 19,800 seats for basketball.*
- *The arena covers 665,000 square feet (62,000 square meters).*
- *The Raptors played their first game in the arena on February 21, 1999.*
- *The arena's new high-definition scoreboard has 17 video screens.*

The Raptors host the New Jersey Nets for a playoff game during the 2006–07 season.

Dressed for Success

The Raptors joined the NBA with four team colors—purple, red, black, and Naismith silver. The name of the last color honors Dr. James Naismith. He was a Canadian educator who *invented* basketball in the 1890s.

In 2003, the team began wearing a red and white uniform for some road games. This was very popular with fans because red and white are the national colors of Canada. In 2006–07, red became the team's main color.

The name Raptors was chosen from more than 2,000 suggestions from fans in a 1994 contest. That same year, *Jurassic Park* was a very popular movie. The team's *logo* shows a red raptor dribbling a basketball. The team uses another logo that shows a basketball surrounded by a three-clawed raptor fossil.

Tracy McGrady shows off Toronto's old purple uniform.

The basketball uniform is very simple. It consists of a roomy top and baggy shorts.

- The top hangs from the shoulders, with big "scoops" for the arms and neck. This style has not changed much over the years.

- Shorts, however, have changed a lot. They used to be very short, so players could move their legs freely. In the last 20 years, shorts have actually gotten longer and much baggier.

Basketball uniforms look the same as they did long ago ... until you look very closely. In the old days, the shorts had belts and buckles. The tops were made of a thick cotton called "jersey," which got very heavy when players sweated. Later, uniforms were made of shiny *satin*. They may have looked great, but they did not "breathe." Players got very hot! Today, most uniforms are made of *synthetic* materials that soak up sweat and keep the body cool.

Jose Calderon brings the ball upcourt in Toronto's 2007–08 road uniform.

We Won!

The Raptors made their first trip to the playoffs in the spring of 2000. They played the New York Knicks, who swept them in three games. Unhappy with this result, the team hired Lenny Wilkens as its new coach.

Wilkens made some important changes during the 2000–01 season.

He moved Vince Carter from forward to guard and replaced him in the frontcourt with rookie Morris Peterson. Wilkens also gave more playing time to Alvin Williams, who became the team's point guard. He turned out to be one of the most dependable players in the NBA. Meanwhile, Carter loved his new position. He averaged 27.6 points a game.

The Raptors kept making changes during the year. They traded for hard-working forward Jerome Williams, who played great defense. They also traded for Keon Clark, a shot-blocking machine. Clark and Charles Oakley combined with Antonio Davis to make Toronto one of the league's best rebounding teams. The Raptors finished the year with 19 wins in their last 27 games. That gave them 47 wins for the season—their best record ever.

As luck would have it, the Raptors faced the Knicks again in the playoffs. The teams had become fierce *rivals* since Toronto joined the NBA. How fierce? The first time Carter touched the ball in the series, Kurt Thomas slammed him to the floor. Carter was exhausted by the end of the game, and the Knicks were able to pull away with a 92–85 win.

Carter took the loss with a sense of humor. "My mom always told me there'll be days like this," he said. "As a matter of fact, she just told me that!"

Carter was all business for Game 2. The Raptors took it to the Knicks and destroyed them in New York, 94–74. It was Toronto's

LEFT: The team's 2000–01 media guide—featuring Vince Carter and Lenny Wilkens—gives fans a hint of great things to come.
ABOVE: Carter drives to the basket in Game 2 against New York Knicks.

first-ever playoff victory. Carter took control of the game in the second half and finished with 22 points. Toronto's defense was excellent. Carter and Williams shut down Latrell Sprewell and Allan Houston, New York's two main scorers.

The Knicks were a tough team. They traveled to Toronto and won Game 3. That meant the Raptors had to win the last two games to take the series. Game 4 began with a windmill dunk by Carter. The fans in Toronto jumped to their feet and stayed there all game as the Raptors won 100–93. Carter had 32 points, and Chris Childs, a **substitute** guard, scored 25.

The two teams returned to New York for Game 5. The Raptors were rebounding monsters. They outjumped the Knicks for almost every missed shot. Toronto built a good lead during the second half. But Sprewell played well, and the Knicks made a **comeback**. New York pulled within two points late in the game.

Wilkens told his players it was "do or die" time. They listened and shut down the Knicks. Toronto opened an eight-point lead and held on for a 93–89 victory.

"We saw this as a good opportunity to make a name for this **franchise**," Carter said after the game. "As a team, and personally, we grew together and brought each other along together."

Carter was brilliant in Toronto's next series, against the Philadelphia

76ers. He and Allen Iverson were locked in a scoring battle that came down to the final shot in Game 7. Carter's game-winning try rolled off the rim to end the Raptors' season. Toronto fans soon realized just how close their team had come to doing the impossible. The 76ers went all the way to the **NBA Finals**.

LEFT: Chris Childs, the hero of Game 3.   **ABOVE**: Jerome Williams celebrates after Toronto's series victory over the Knicks.

Go-To Guys

To be a true star in the NBA, you need more than a great shot. You have to be a "go-to guy"—someone teammates trust to make the winning play when the seconds are ticking away in a big game. Raptors fans have had a lot to cheer about over the years, including these great stars …

THE PIONEERS

DAMON STOUDAMIRE   5´ 10˝ Guard

• BORN: 9/3/1973   • PLAYED FOR TEAM: 1995–96 TO 1997–98

As a boy, Damon Stoudamire looked to Nate "Tiny" Archibald as his idol. Like Archibald, Stoudamire became an All-Star. He topped the Raptors in scoring and assists all three years he played for them. In 1996, he set a team record with 19 assists in a game.

DOUG CHRISTIE   6´ 6˝ Guard

• BORN: 5/9/1970

• PLAYED FOR TEAM: 1995–96 TO 1999–00

Doug Christie sat on the bench for other teams until the Raptors gave him a chance to play. Christie took the opportunity to learn about the **professional** game. Before long, he proved he could be a good scorer and an excellent defender in the NBA.

MARCUS CAMBY 6´ 11˝ Center

- Born: 3/22/1974
- Played for Team: 1996–97 to 1997–98

The Raptors selected Marcus Camby with the second pick in the 1996 draft. He was a good rebounder and shot-blocker during his two seasons with the team. Camby showed that quickness and defense were keys to winning in the NBA.

TRACY McGRADY 6´ 8˝ Guard/Forward

- Born: 5/24/1979   • Played for Team: 1997–98 to 1999–00

Tracy McGrady went right from high school to the NBA. In his first year as a starter, he helped Toronto make the playoffs for the first time. "T-Mac" averaged 15 points and six rebounds that year.

ALVIN WILLIAMS 6´ 5˝ Guard

- Born: 8/6/1974   • Played for Team: 1997–98 to 2005–06

A winning team needs **role players** as well as stars. Alvin Williams understood this better than anyone. He came to play every night and gave the Raptors whatever they needed to win.

VINCE CARTER 6´ 6˝ Guard/Forward

- Born: 1/26/1977   • Played for Team: 1998–99 to 2004–05

Vince Carter was the most talented player to wear a Toronto uniform. He could leap over defenders for thunderous dunks. He could hit 25-foot jump shots. And he was at his best when everyone was watching him. Carter was the NBA Slam Dunk champion in 2000 and tied a playoff record with nine **3-pointers** in a game in 2001.

LEFT: Damon Stoudamire   **ABOVE**: Marcus Camby

MODERN STARS

ANTONIO DAVIS   6´ 9˝ Forward

• BORN: 10/31/1968   • PLAYED FOR TEAM: 1999–00 TO 2003–04 & 2005–06

Antonio Davis brought playoff experience to the Raptors. Toronto made it to the **postseason** in each of his first three years with the team. In 2000–01, he played in the All-Star Game for the first time in his career.

MORRIS PETERSON   6´ 7˝ Guard/Forward

• BORN: 8/26/1977

• PLAYED FOR TEAM: 2000–01 TO 2006–07

Morris Peterson was one of the most popular Raptors ever. He drove opponents crazy with his defense and brought the fans to their feet with his amazing shots. The lefty could hit long shots from the outside and go high for rebounds.

JALEN ROSE 6´ 8˝ Guard/Forward

• BORN: 1/30/1973

• PLAYED FOR TEAM: 2003–04 TO 2005–06

When Jalen Rose joined the Raptors, they asked him to play three different positions. He did that and more. Rose was a super-smooth shooter and passer who often scored 20 points a game.

ABOVE: Jalen Rose   **RIGHT**: Chris Bosh and Andrea Bargnani

CHRIS BOSH 6′ 10″ Forward

- BORN: 3/24/1984
- FIRST SEASON WITH TEAM: 2003–04

Young players often take years to learn the ins and outs of the NBA. Chris Bosh did it much faster than that. He studied the pro game and memorized the moves of his opponents. Bosh used his sharp mind, soft hands, and quick feet to become a star.

ANDREA BARGNANI
7′ 0″ Forward

- BORN: 10/26/1985
- FIRST SEASON WITH TEAM: 2006–07

Italian-born Andrea Bargnani was the first player chosen in the 2006 draft. He looked like a center but had the shooting and driving skills of a small forward. In his rookie season, Bargnani helped the Raptors win their first **division** championship.

JERMAINE O'NEAL 6′ 11″ Forward

- BORN: 10/13/1978 • FIRST SEASON WITH TEAM: 2008–09

The Raptors have had good luck with experienced **power forwards** and centers. When they had a chance to get Jermaine O'Neal from the Indiana Pacers, they didn't think twice. O'Neal was an All-Star six times and averaged 24 points a game in 2004–05.

On the Sidelines

T he Raptors' first two coaches were Brendan Malone and Darrell Walker. Their job was to build a solid foundation for the future. Toronto's next coach, Butch Carter, had been an assistant to Walker. When Carter took over, he promised the fans he would lead Toronto to the playoffs. In 1999–00, the Raptors finished with 43 victories and reached the postseason for the first time.

Toronto's next coach was Lenny Wilkens. At the time, Toronto had many skilled players, but the team lacked confidence. Wilkens got the Raptors to believe in themselves and created a winning feeling in the locker room. Under Wilkens, Toronto became one of the toughest teams in the **Eastern Conference**. Wilkens was followed by Kevin O'Neill, who was a graduate of Canada's McGill University.

In 2004, the Raptors hired Sam Mitchell to be their coach. Mitchell helped the club rebuild and led Toronto to the **Atlantic Division** championship in 2006–07. He was named NBA **Coach of the Year**. The following season, he became the team's all-time winningest coach.

Lenny Wilkens draws up a play for the Raptors during a 2002–03 game.

One Great Day

Fans who bought tickets for the 2001 **Eastern Conference Semifinals** expected to see a scoring battle between Toronto's Vince Carter and Allen Iverson of the Philadelphia 76ers. They were not disappointed. Carter scored 35 in Game 1 for the Raptors. Iverson scored 54 in Game 2. When the series moved from Philadelphia to Toronto, Raptors fans had high expectations for Carter.

Carter was up to the challenge. He came out shooting in the first quarter and made one basket after another. With each shot, the rim looked bigger and bigger to Carter. He scored 15 of Toronto's first 19 points. He continued his hot shooting. After 22 minutes, he had 34 points.

Twenty-four of those points came on 3-point shots. Carter took nine in the first half and made eight. That set a new league playoff record for 3-pointers in one half. Carter made another 3-pointer in the second half to tie the league record for a playoff game.

By then the Raptors were in total control. Carter was playing the best game of his career. Besides his amazing scoring—he finished

Vince Carter dunks during his amazing 50-point performance against the Philadelphia 76ers in the 2001 playoffs.

with 50 points—Carter had six rebounds, seven assists, and four blocked shots.

His greatest contribution came on defense. When Alvin Williams and Chris Childs failed to stop Iverson, Carter moved over and shut him down. That helped Toronto win easily, 102–78.

"Vince Carter was *sensational* tonight," Toronto coach Lenny Wilkens said. "He had that look in his eye before the game. He put on an incredible show in the first half."

Carter agreed. "I came out focused and ready to play," he said.

Legend Has It

Which Raptor got his nickname from a cartoon character?

LEGEND HAS IT that Damon Stoudamire did. Stoudamire was one of the toughest, fastest, most talented players in the NBA. Though he stood less than six feet, he played with the power and

energy of someone much taller. Fans and teammates called him "Mighty Mouse." He liked the name so much that he got a tattoo of the cartoon character on his arm. Stoudamire was the shortest player ever to be named **Rookie of the Year**.

ABOVE: Damon Stoudamire shows off his 1996 Rookie of the Year trophy.
RIGHT: All in the family—Tracy McGrady and Vince Carter.

Which Toronto stars were third cousins?

LEGEND HAS IT that Vince Carter and Tracy McGrady were. The two stars first met at a game when McGrady was in high school and Carter was in college. They became friends, but did not know they were related. At a family *reunion* in Florida, they discovered that their grandmothers were first cousins. That made McGrady and Carter third cousins.

Were the Raptors almost called the Hogs?

LEGEND HAS IT that they were. When it came time to choose a name for the team, many fans wanted to go back to Toronto's first pro team, the Huskies. But the NBA thought this would be too much like the Timberwolves, who played in Minnesota. A contest was held and the choices were Beavers, Bobcats, Dragons, Grizzlies, Raptors, Scorpions, T-Rex, Tarantulas, Terriers, and Hogs.

It Really Happened

When an NBA team makes big changes in the middle of a season, no one can be certain that the club will improve. During the 2000–01 season, the Raptors brought in several new players. Toronto hoped to improve its defense. Not in their wildest dreams did the Raptors imagine how much better they would become.

One of the newcomers was Keon Clark. He was a rail-thin forward who could jump 40 inches in the air. He used his long arms like fly swatters when an opponent tried to score on him.

In a game against the Atlanta Hawks, Clark went wild. It was like watching a video game. The Hawks kept shooting, and Clark kept rejecting their shots. Soon his teammates got in on the fun. When the final buzzer sounded, the Raptors had set an NBA record with 23 blocks.

Clark had more than half of the team's blocked shots with 12. That broke the team record of 11, which was held by Marcus Camby. The amazing thing is that Clark did not start the game— he came off the bench!

All five Toronto starters finished with at least one blocked shot. Vince Carter had four, while Jerome Williams and Alvin Williams had two each. The Raptors won the game easily, 112–86.

Keon Clark rises to block a shot during the 2000–01 season.

After the game, Clark reminded reporters that the victory was more important than setting the record. "As long as we won," he said, "it didn't matter if I got two blocks or twelve."

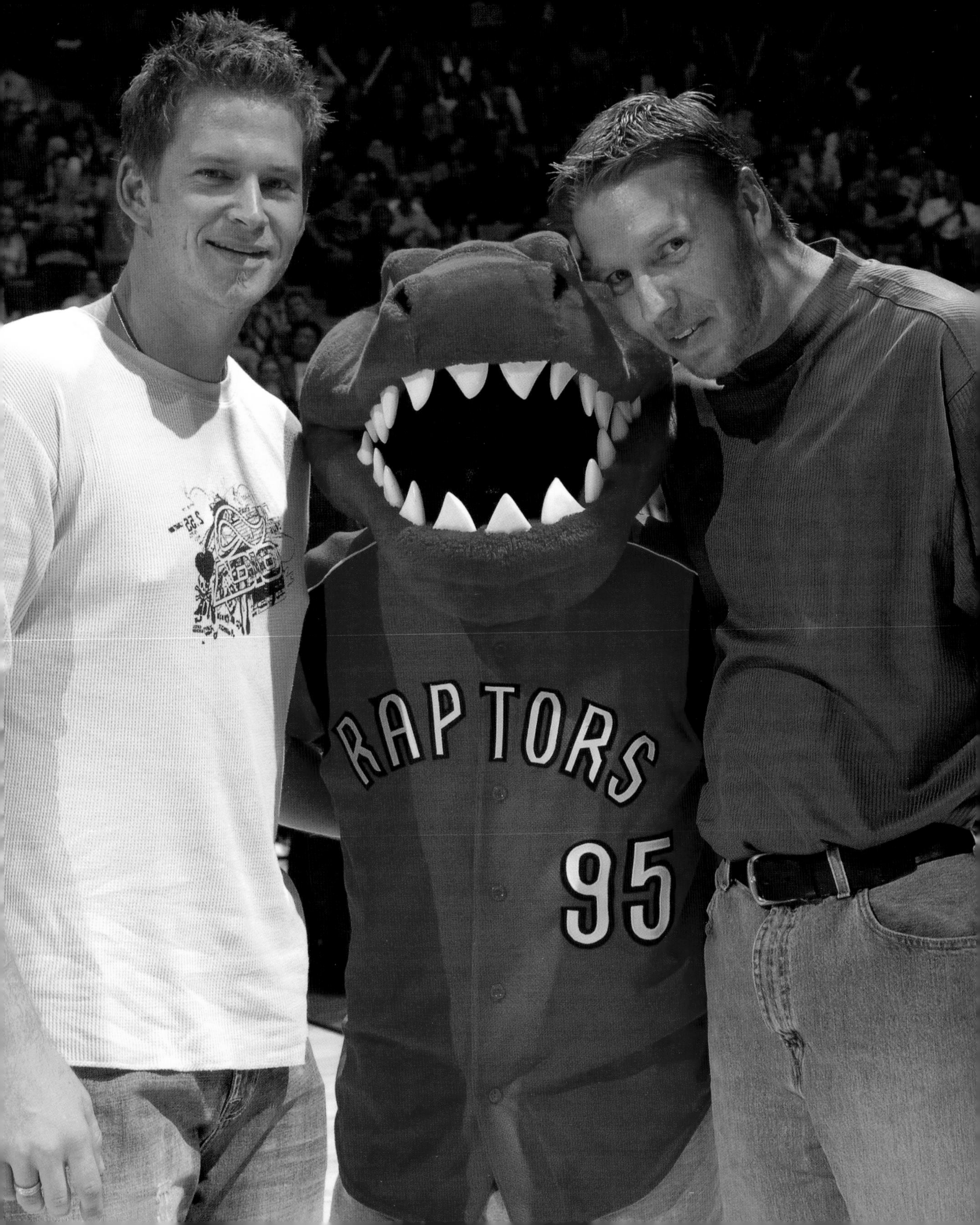
RAPTORS
95

Team Spirit

When the NBA decided to place a team in Toronto, many wondered whether Canadian fans would support basketball—even though it was invented by a Canadian and the league's first game was played in Toronto between the Huskies and the New York Knicks. They didn't need to worry. The Raptors have played in front of large crowds year after year.

The Raptors reward their fans with exciting basketball, first-rate food, and lots of free souvenirs and events. During games, the team turns up the volume with the Raptors Dance Pak and 4 Korners Raptors Soundcrew. The team *mascot*, a big red dinosaur, is one of the coolest in the NBA.

Between games, the "Raps" go out into the community to mix with their fans. Toronto players appear at charity events throughout the *province* of Ontario and support programs for making smart choices in life. Since their first season, the Raptors have raised nearly $20 million for charitable causes.

A.J. Burnett and Roy Halladay of the Blue Jays baseball team pose for a picture with Raptor. Fans love the Toronto mascot.

Timeline

The basketball season is played from October through June. That means each season takes place at the end of one year and the beginning of the next. In this timeline, the accomplishments of the Raptors are shown by season.

1995–96
The Raptors
join the NBA.

1997–98
The Raptors draft
18-year-old Tracy McGrady.

1992–93
The NBA announces plans to
place a new team in Toronto.

1996–97
Doug Christie is second
in the league in steals.

The media guide
from Toronto's
first season.

Doug
Christie

Vince
Carter

Kevin Willis, a
key player for the
2000–01 team.

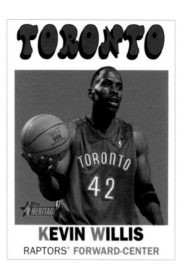

1999–00
Vince Carter is the first Raptor
to start in the All-Star Game.

2000–01
The Raptors block
23 shots in a game.

1998–99
The Raptors move
into their new arena.

2003–04
Donyell Marshall gets
24 rebounds in a game.

2007–08
Jason Kapono wins
the 3-Point Shootout.

Jason Kapono sizes
up a shot during his
victory in the 2008
3-Point Shootout.

Fun Facts

STORYBOOK CAREER

Chris Bosh loved to read in high school. He was a member of the *National Honor Society*. Today, Bosh and his mother read a book a month, and then call each other to discuss it when they are done.

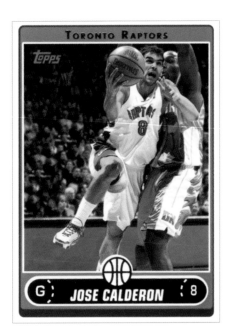

SURE HANDS

In 2007–08, Jose Calderon was asked to replace injured T.J. Ford as the Raptors' point guard. The Spanish star had 5.38 assists for every **turnover** he committed. This was the best mark in the NBA.

CLEAN SWEEP

In January of 2007, the Raptors had the NBA's Player of the Month (Chris Bosh), Rookie of the Month (Andrea Bargnani), and Coach of the Month (Sam Mitchell). It was the first time a team ever won all three awards in the same month.

ABOVE: Jose Calderon
RIGHT: Donyell Marshall launches one of his record 12 3-pointers.

TRIPLE TROUBLE

In a 2005 game against the Philadelphia 76ers, the Raptors set an NBA record for 3-pointers with 21. Donyell Marshall tied a record by making 12. When the 2008–09 season started, the Raptors had made 3-pointers in 776 games in a row. This was also an NBA record.

INTO AFRICA

Toronto's longtime assistant coach Alex English leads a group of NBA players across the Atlantic Ocean each summer to work with young players from Africa. It is part of the Basketball Without Borders program. English first became interested in Africa in 1985. That year he convinced his fellow All-Stars to donate money to buy food for people starving in Ethiopia.

CARTER COUNTRY

Toronto's third coach, Butch Carter, was the big brother of football star Cris Carter. Butch starred for the University of Indiana's basketball team in the 1970s. Cris starred for Ohio State University's football team in the 1980s.

Talking Hoops

"Leaders set the tone for their **peers**. Peers look up to them and say, 'They're doing it, so I'm doing it.'"
—*Chris Bosh, on what it takes to be a leader*

"There are a lot of talented guys around the NBA who don't care about winning. This guy wants to win."
—*Loren Woods, on teammate Chris Bosh*

"I like to smile, even in intense situations. My opponents don't know how to react when they see me smile."
—*Vince Carter, on why he is successful in pressure situations*

"Show people how to have success and then you can push their expectations up."
—*Lenny Wilkens, on the key to winning in the NBA*

"In order to do great things, you have to take on challenges in your life."
—Tracy McGrady, on how to become an NBA star

"There's 82 games and definitely enough minutes … it's for the good of the team to spread the minutes around."
—Anthony Parker, on sharing playing time with his teammates

"I want all our guys who can shoot to shoot the ball when they're open."
—Sam Mitchell, on his coaching philosophy

LEFT: Chris Bosh
ABOVE: Anthony Parker

For the Record

The great Raptors teams and players have left their marks on the record books. These are the "best of the best" …

WINNER	AWARD	SEASON
Damon Stoudamire	Rookie of the Year	1995–96
Vince Carter	Rookie of the Year	1998–99
Vince Carter	Slam Dunk Champion	1999–00
Sam Mitchell	Coach of the Year	2006–07
Jason Kapono	3-Point Shootout Champion	2007–08

RAPTORS AWARD WINNERS

ABOVE: The Raptors celebrate with Sam Mitchell after his Coach of the Year award.   **RIGHT**: Vince Carter eyes the rim during the 2000 Slam Dunk Contest.

Pinpoints

The history of a basketball team is made up of many smaller stories. These stories take place all over the map—not just in the city a team calls "home." Match the push-pins on these maps to the Team Facts and you will begin to see the story of the Raptors unfold!

TEAM FACTS

1   Hartford, Connecticut—*Marcus Camby was born here.*

2   Philadelphia, Pennsylvania—*Alvin Williams was born here.*

3   Columbus, Georgia—*Sam Mitchell was born here.*

4   Bartow, Florida—*Tracy McGrady was born here.*

5   Danville, Illinois—*Keon Clark was born here.*

6   Dallas, Texas—*Chris Bosh was born here.*

7   Oakland, California—*Antonio Davis was born here.*

8   Portland, Oregon—*Damon Stoudamire was born here.*

9   Seattle, Washington—*Doug Christie was born here.*

10   Toronto, Ontario, Canada—*The Raptors have played here since 1995–96.*

11   Rome, Italy—*Andrea Bargnani was born here.*

12   Villanueva de la Serena, Spain—*Jose Calderon was born here.*

Alvin Williams

Play Ball

Basketball is a sport played by two teams of five players. NBA games have four 12-minute quarters—48 minutes in all—and the team that scores the most points when time has run out is the winner. Most baskets count for two points. Players who make shots from beyond the three-point line receive an extra point. Baskets made from the free-throw line count for one point. Free throws are penalty shots awarded to a team, usually after an opponent has committed a foul. A foul is called when one player makes hard contact with another.

Players can move around all they want, but the player with the ball cannot. He must bounce the ball with one hand or the other (but never both) in order to go from one part of the court to another. As long as he keeps "dribbling," he can keep moving.

In the NBA, teams must attempt a shot every 24 seconds, so there is little time to waste. The job of the defense is to make it as difficult as possible to take a good shot—and to grab the ball if the other team shoots and misses.

This may sound simple, but anyone who has played the game knows that basketball can be very complicated. Every player on the court has a job to do. Different players have different strengths and weaknesses. The coach must mix these players in just the right way, and teach them to work together as one.

The more you play and watch basketball, the more "little things" you are likely to notice. The next time you are at a game, look for these plays:

ALLEY-OOP—A play where the passer throws the ball just to the side of the rim—so a teammate can catch it and dunk in one motion.

BACK-DOOR PLAY—A play where the passer waits for his teammate to fake the defender away from the basket—then throws him the ball when he cuts back toward the basket.

KICK-OUT—A play where the ball-handler waits for the defense to surround him—then quickly passes to a teammate who is open for an outside shot. The ball is not really kicked in this play; the term comes from the action of pinball machines.

NO-LOOK PASS—A play where the passer fools a defender (with his eyes) into covering one teammate—then suddenly passes to another without looking.

PICK-AND-ROLL—A play where one teammate blocks or "picks off" another's defender with his body—then cuts to the basket for a pass in the confusion.

Glossary

BASKETBALL WORDS TO KNOW

3-POINTERS—Baskets made from behind the 3-point line.

ALL-STAR—A player selected to play in the annual All-Star Game.

ALL-STAR GAME—The annual game in which the best players from the East and the West play against each other. The game does not count in the standings.

ASSISTS—Passes that lead to successful shots.

ATLANTIC DIVISION—A group of teams that plays in the northeast part of the country.

COACH OF THE YEAR—An award given each season to the league's best coach.

COMEBACK—The process of catching up from behind, or making up a large deficit.

DIVISION—A group of teams within a league that play in the same part of the country.

DRAFT CHOICE—A college player selected or "drafted" by an NBA team each summer.

EASTERN CONFERENCE—A group of teams that play in the East. The winner of the Eastern Conference meets the winner of the Western Conference in the league finals.

EASTERN CONFERENCE SEMIFINALS—The playoff series that determines which two teams will play each other for the Eastern Conference Championship.

EXPANSION TEAMS—New teams that join a league already in business.

FRANCHISE—The business people and players who make up a sports team.

NATIONAL BASKETBALL ASSOCIATION (NBA)—The professional league that has been operating since 1946–47.

NBA DRAFT—The annual meeting where teams pick from a group of the best college players.

NBA FINALS—The playoff series that decides the champion of the league.

PLAYOFFS—The games played after the season to determine the league champion.

POSTSEASON—Another term for playoffs.

POWER FORWARDS—The bigger and stronger of a team's forwards.

PROFESSIONAL—A player or team that plays a sport for money. College players are not paid, so they are considered "amateurs."

ROLE PLAYERS—People who are asked to do specific things when they are in a game.

ROOKIE—A player in his first season.

ROOKIE OF THE YEAR—The annual award given to the league's best first-year player.

ROSTER—The list of players on a team.

SUBSTITUTE—A player who begins most games on the bench.

TEAM CHEMISTRY—The ability of teammates to work together well. Winning teams often have good team chemistry.

TURNOVER—A play in which the team on offense loses possession of the ball.

OTHER WORDS TO KNOW

CENTURY—A period of 100 years.

CULTURAL DIVERSITY—The mix of people and customs from different ethnic backgrounds.

ERA—A period of time in history.

INTERNATIONAL—From all over the world.

INVENTED—Created through clever thinking.

LOGO—A symbol or design that represents a company or team.

MASCOT—An animal or person believed to bring a group good luck.

NATIONAL HONOR SOCIETY—An organization that recognizes the top students in high school and lower education levels.

OUTSMARTED—Got the better of by being clever.

OVERLOOKED—Had a view from above.

PEERS—People of equal standing.

PROVINCE—A specific region in Canada that is similar to a state.

RETRACTABLE—Able to pull back.

REUNION—A gathering of friends or family.

RIVALS—Extremely emotional competitors.

SATIN—A smooth, shiny fabric.

SENSATIONAL—Amazing.

SYNTHETIC—Made in a laboratory, not in nature.

UPBEAT—Cheerful and excited.

Places to Go

ON THE ROAD

TORONTO RAPTORS
40 Bay Street
Toronto, Ontario M5J-2N8 Canada
(416) 815-5600

NAISMITH MEMORIAL BASKETBALL HALL OF FAME
1000 West Columbus Avenue
Springfield, Massachusetts 01105
(877) 4HOOPLA

ON THE WEB

THE NATIONAL BASKETBALL ASSOCIATION   www.nba.com
  • *Learn more about the league's teams, players, and history*

THE TORONTO RAPTORS   www.nba.com/raptors/
  • *Learn more about the Raptors*

THE BASKETBALL HALL OF FAME   www.hoophall.com
  • *Learn more about history's greatest players*

ON THE BOOKSHELF

To learn more about the sport of basketball, look for these books at your library or bookstore:

  • Hareas, John. *Basketball*. New York, New York: DK, 2005.

  • Hughes, Morgan. *Basketball*. Vero Beach, Florida: Rourke Publishing, 2005.

  • Thomas, Keltie. *How Basketball Works*. Berkeley, California: Maple Tree Press, distributed through Publishers Group West, 2005.

Index

The Team

MARK STEWART has written more than 20 books on basketball, and over 100 sports books for kids. He grew up in New York City during the 1960s rooting for the Knicks and Nets, and now takes his two daughters, Mariah and Rachel, to watch them play. Mark comes from a family of writers. His grandfather was Sunday Editor of *The New York Times* and his mother was Articles Editor of *The Ladies Home Journal* and *McCall's*. Mark has profiled hundreds of athletes over the last 20 years. He has also written several books about his native New York, and New Jersey, his home today. Mark is a graduate of Duke University, with a degree in history. He lives with his daughters and wife, Sarah, overlooking Sandy Hook, New Jersey.

MATT ZEYSING is the resident historian at the Basketball Hall of Fame in Springfield, Massachusetts. His research interests include the origins of the game of basketball, the development of professional basketball in the first half of the twentieth century, and the culture and meaning of basketball in American society.